I0157251

My Christmas Song Collection

Lyrics
&
Scores
By
Richard Mousseau

MOOSE HIDE BOOKS
imprint of
MOOSE ENTERPRISE PUBLISHING
**PRINCE TOWNSHIP
ONTARIO, CANADA**

cover illustration by Rick Mousseau

My Christmas Song Collection
Lyrics & Scores By
Richard Mousseau
Copyright November 1, 2021

Published Dec 1, 2021
by

MOOSE HIDE BOOKS
imprint of
MOOSE ENTERPRISE PUBLISHING
684 WALLS ROAD
PRINCE TOWNSHIP
ONTARIO, CANADA
P6A 6K4
web site www.moosehidebooks.com

NO VENTURE UNATTAINABLE

ALL RIGHTS RESERVED, NO PART OF THIS BOOK MAY BE REPRODUCED, THIS INCLUDES STORING IN RETRIEVAL SYSTEM OR TRANSMITTED IN ANY FORM BY ELECTRONIC MEANS, MECHANICAL, PHOTOCOPYING, RECORDING OR OTHER, WITHOUT THE WRITTEN PERMISSION FROM THIS PUBLISHER.
ALL COMPOSITIONS HOLD INDIVIDUAL COPYRIGHT AND IS NOTED ON EACH TITLE PAGE. THIS BOOK IS A COLLECTION OF THE AUTHOR'S WORKS. PURCHASERS OF THESE MUSICAL COMPOSITIONS ARE ENTITLED TO USE FOR PERSONAL USE. HOWEVER, DUPLICATION, ADAPTATION, ARRANGEMENT AND OR PUBLIC PERFORMANCES, OR TRANSMISSION OF SAID COMPOSITIONS OF COPYRIGHTED MATERIAL REQUIRES THE WRITTEN CONSENT OF THE COPYRIGHT OWNERS. UNAUTHORIZED USES ARE INFRINGEMENTS OF THE COPYRIGHT LAWS ADOPTED WORLD-WIDE, AND MAY SUBJECT THE USER TO CIVIL AND CRIMINAL PENALTIES.

CREATED IN CANADA

Library and Archives Canada Cataloguing in Publication

Includes Index.

Mousseau, Richard 1953-Author of lyrics & Musical Scores
        My Christmas Song Collection / Richard Mousseau

Issued in print and electronic formats.
ISBN 978-1-927393-71-0(pbk.). - -ISBN 978-1-927393-72-7(pdf)

        I. Title.

Table Of Contents

My Christmas Song Collection

A Christmas Of White

Lyrics by
Richard Mousseau

Score by
Richard Mousseau

Lyrics:

When the snow cov-ers the pines, and wint-er winds blow. I'll re-call our walks be-neath norther-en lights a-glow. A Christ-mas of white fills my dream, and trees with pret-ty lights all a-gleam. In the park we hear sligh bells ring. On this Christ-mas night An-gels sing. We wish you a mer-ry Christ-mas and a joy the sea-son through. Un-til we meet next Christ-mas.

Copyright September 28, 2021, Moose Hide Publishing
imprint of Moose Enterprise Book and Theatre Play Publishing
All rights reserved
684 Walls Rd. Prince Twp., Ontario Canada P6A 6K4
mooseenterprises@on.aibn.com www.moosehidebooks.com

may your hopes and wish - es all come true.

A Christ - mas of white fills my dream, and trees with pret - ty lights all a - gleam. In the park we hear sligh bells ring. On this Christ-mas night An-gels sing. We wish you a mer-ry Christ - mas and a joy the sea-son through. Un - til we meet next Christ - mas. may your hopes and wish - es all come true. We wish you a mer-ry Christ - mas - .

May your hopes and wish - es all come

true.

A Kiss Beneath The Mistletoe

Lyrics by
Richard Mousseau

Score by
Richard Mousseau

♩=110

Intro

met a lit-tle girl with eyes so ev-er green, the pret-ti-est one I've ev-er seen. She told me bold-ly

not to look at her for I'm not the boy she would per-fer to kiss be-

neath the mis-tle-toe. I told the lit-tle girl she

was just right for me for this is just the way life has to be, and when we are old-er

Copyright December 7, 2018, Moose Hide Publishing
imprint of Moose Enterprise Book and Theatre Play Publishing
All rights reserved
684 Walls Rd. Prince Twp., Ontario Canada P6A 6K4
mooseenterprises@on.aibn.com www.moosehidebooks.com

she will then know that some day soon I'd be her beau, and kiss be-neath the mis-tle-

toe.

Each New Years Eve I would of-ten seek, and try to kiss her ros-y cheek, then

one new year true love came our way, and this is all I have to say, we kissed be-

neath the mis-tle-toe. Many years have passed since

our first kiss, and our true love will not re-sist last-ing through the years un-till old and gray, and

9

75   F   E♭   B♭   Gm   C   F

I am glad we can now say, we kissed be - neath the mis - tle - toe.

80   Faug   B♭   VF5   C

And now I wait un-under the mis - lte - toe, re -

84   F   E♭   B♭   F   C

mem -bering her smile so many years a - go, and wait-ing for a kiss from a lit - tle girl

88   G   D   Gm   F   C

I use to know when I was just a lad. When

93   Gm   F >   F >   C >   F
End

I was just a lad.

97   C⁷   F   B♭ >   F >   F >

A New Year's Eve Date

(Auld Lang Syne interlude)

Lyrics and Score by
Richard Mousseau

Interlude words by
Robert Burns
Traditional Music

Holiday New Year's Eve Song

If I on-ly had the nerve and bold en-ough to state that you and I per-haps should need to test our fate on a first date New Year's Eve.

Do you have an in-vita-tion, I'm ask-ing with spite, will some-one else be hold-ing you nice and tight on a first date New Year's Eve.

I must be a fool to ev-er ex-pect from the man-y Beaus you could se-lect, I would be the one, and on-ly one, you would pick. If

Copyright November 25, 2018, Moose Hide Publishing
imprint of Moose Enterprise Book and Theatre Play Publishing
All rights reserved
684 Walls Rd. Prince Twp., Ontario Canada P6A 6K4
mooseenterprises@on.aibn.com www.moosehidebooks.com

27 F V 3 / Gm / Am / Gm

on-ly dreams came true, and I was hold-ing you, would we be-gin to dance, and take a chance

31 C F Bb C C6 F Interlude C7

on a first date New Year's Eve. Should auld ac-quaint-ance be for-got, and

37 F F7 Bb F C7 Am Dm Gm7 C7

nev-er brought to mind. Should auld ac-quaint-ance be for-got and days of Auld Lang

42 F C7 F C7 F F7 Bb

Syne. For Auld - Lang - Syne, my derar, for Auld - Lang - Syne. We'll

47 F C7 Am Dm Gm7 C7 F Gm

tak' a cup o' kind - ness yet, for - Auld - Lang - Syne. If I

51 F V 1 Gm Am

on - ly had the nerve and bold en-ough to state that you and I per-haps should

54 Gm C F Bb C C6 F Bb

need to test our fate on a first date New Year's Eve. I

59 Eb Bb Eb Bb
Chorus

must be a fool to ev - er ex-pect from the man -y Beaus you could se-lect,

63
C Am C Am G C C7
I would be the one, and on - ly one, you would pick. If
3
67
F V 3 Gm Am Gm
on-ly dreams came true, and I was hold-ing you, would we be-gin to dance, and take a chance
71
C F B♭ C C6 F C7
on a first date New Year's Eve.
Instrumental End
77
F F7 B♭ F C7 Am Dm Gm7 C7 F

A New-Year's Kiss

Lyrics by
Richard Mousseau

Score by
Richard Mousseau

♩=100 *Holiday Song*

Intro

V 1
past, I re-call a New-Year's kiss, from a strang-er, to this day I still

miss. Just a girl with a smile that said hel-lo to a stang-er that she

wished would be her beau. Time stood

V 2
still while I held my lips u-pon a strang-er's kiss, I wished would go

on. New-Year's Eve be-neath a Mist-le-toe, my strang-er holds me

close, her smile a-glow.

Copyright December 29, 2019, Moose Hide Publishing
imprint of Moose Enterprise Book and Theatre Play Publishing
All rights reserved
684 Walls Rd. Prince Twp., Ontario Canada P6A 6K4
mooseenterprises@on.aibn.com www.moosehidebooks.com

Each New-Year's Eve, a vission of her I see. A stang-er re-turns to me be-neath the Mist-le-toe.

Each New-Year's Eve, a vission of her I see. A stang-er re-turns to me be-neath the Mist-le-toe. Just a girl with a smile that said hel-lo to a stang-er that she wished would be her beau. From my past, I re-call a New-Year's kiss, from a

strang - er, to this day I still miss.

3

16

A Shepherd

Lyrics by
Richard Mousseau

Score by
Richard Mousseau

Intro / V.1: From on high I see a star shine bright. I do won - der where it leads me this night. Fol - low me say I, to a wear - y flock of sheep. This night is cold and we shall not sleep.

V.2: I am just a poor young shep - herd. On this night I seek fair warmth for my herd. Fol - low me say I for warmth and hay a - waits. A co - zy man - ger shall be our fate.

V.3: As we bed u - pon the hay this night, in from the cold stang - ers here we in -

Copyright December 17, 2019, Moose Hide Publishing
imprint of Moose Enterprise Book and Theatre Play Publishing
All rights reserved
684 Walls Rd. Prince Twp., Ontario Canada P6A 6K4
mooseenterprises@on.aibn.com www.moosehidebooks.com

vite. Rest thee gent-ly, I see that you are with child. A - mong us be safe here from the wild. Of my - self I give to serve your need. In this man - ger, man and beast we do cede. Rest thee gent-ly bring forth birth a child so pure, and hope vile ways will not be en - dured. On this night wize men fol - low a star, bar - ing gifts for a sav - ior born a - far. In a man - ger lies a child in Beth - le - ham, to rise a - bove the li - on lies a lamb. I am just a shep - herd of no worth. On this night I bare wit - ness to a birth. In a man - ger lies a babe in Beth - le - ham, to rise a-bove the li - on lies a

lamb. In a man - ger lies a babe in Beth le -

ham.

Beneath Mistletoe

Lyrics by
Richard Mousseau

Score by
Richard Mousseau

Holiday Song ♩=110

Intro — V 1 — A — D

A blue heart is stand-ing be-neath mis-tle-toe,
wait-ing for a kiss from a boy who did not show, to a
New-Year's Par-ty a life-time a-go. Though she stayed to wait, he
had reas-ons I know. A cold tear has fall-en from a mist-y
eye. She hopes that no-one would ev-er see her cry.
At the chime of mid-night her torn heart did sigh. Look-ing to the
stars, she would ask heav-en why must young life be so crule, and

Chorus

Copyright November 15, 2018, Moose Hide Publishing
imprint of Moose Enterprise Book and Theatre Play Publishing
All rights reserved
684 Walls Rd. Prince Twp., Ontario Canada P6A 6K4
mooseenterprises@on.aibn.com www.moosehidebooks.com

play her for a fool? Why can't ro-mance come true, why must this night be so

blue.

I stood

by a storm drain be-neath a street light, star-ing down be - low a

grate as dark as night. From my hands a band of gold fell from my

sight. Plead-ing to the stars, I asked why does life spite? Must

young life be so crule, and play her for a fool? Why can't ro-mance come

true, why must this night be so blue? A blue heart is stand-ing be-neath mis - tle - toe, wait-ing for a kiss from a boy who did not

show, Wait - ing for a kiss be -

neath mis - tle - toe.

Christmas Trees

Lyrics by
Richard Mousseau

Score by
Richard Mousseau

Christ-mas trees, I re-mem-ber when I was small, the tops reached up so tall. I re-call Christ-mas day sil-ver bells on boughs would chime, and songs were sung in rhyme. What a time to be so young.

One Christ-mas day, I re-mem-ber a young girl's smile. My lame kiss was fu-tile. I re-call a Christ-mas night, you let me hold your

Copyright Aug 27, 2020, Moose Hide Publishing
imprint of Moose Enterprise Book and Theatre Play Publishing
All rights reserved
684 Walls Rd. Prince Twp., Ontario Canada P6A 6K4
mooseenterprises@on.aibn.com www.moosehidebooks.com

36
A D G♭m Fm G
hand. I prom-ised a wed-ding band. What a time to be so young.
41
G♭m Em F G A
Chorus
Since time has passed on by, those years bring a
46
D G♭m Fm
sigh. I of-ten won-der why, past mem-or-ies make one cry?
51
V 3
G A
This Christ-mas day, I re - mem-ber the years of past. I
55
D G♭m Fm
thought our years would last. I de - test this Christ-mas day. Just
59
G A D G♭m
old mem-or-ies re - main. I wal-low a-lone in vain. What a
63
Fm G G♭m Em F
Chorus
time when we were young. Since time has passed on
68
G A D G♭m
by, those years bring a sigh. I of-ten won-der why, past

mem-or-ies make one cry?   Christ-mas trees,   I re - mem-ber when I was

small,   the tops reached up so tall. I re - call your sweet smile.

25

I remember a Christmas Night

Lyrics by
Richard Mousseau

Score by
Richard Mousseau

Lyrics under the music:

I re-mem-ber a snow-y night when I was once young. Through the win-dow I saw a sight, boughs of green there hung. Fam-ily gather-ed to fill, a home warm-ing night's chill. I re-mem-ber a christ-mas night.

V 2

At mid-night mass the church bells rang, to greet a new-born. A con-gra-ga-tion of voic-es sang, with an an-gel's horn. fam-ilies gather-ed to pray. Child-reren want-ing to play. I re-mem-ber

Copyright December 19, 2017, Moose Hide Publishing
imprint of Moose Enterprise Book and Theatre Play Publishing
All rights reserved
684 Walls Rd. Prince Twp., Ontario Canada P6A 6K4
mooseenterprises@on.aibn.com www.moosehidebooks.com

a christ-mas night.

It is a dam shame to grow old,

to be all a-lone, no fam-ily to sa-vour as gold. This

I must a-tone. Where have all the years gone, as if I don't

be-long? It is a dam shame to grow old.

I re-mem-ber a christ-mass night, when I was once young.

Through the win-dow I saw a sight, boughs of green there hung,

fam-i-ly gather-ed to fill, a home warm-ing night's chill.

I re-mem-ber a christ-mas night.

Let's Go Home

Lyrics by
Richard Mousseau

Score by
Richard Mousseau

Copyright November 27, 2012, Moose Hide Publishing
imprint of Moose Enterprise Book and Theatre Play Publishing
All rights reserved
684 Walls Rd. Prince Twp., Ontario Canada P6A 6K4
mooseenterprises@on.aibn.com www.moosehidebooks.com

key.

I walk crowd-ed streets of pret - ty light-s and see the hap - py

sight-s of peop-le shov - ing me to and frow. Un-til you

take my hand and say dar - ling let's go home where a fire is crack-ling and

egg - nog is sooth -ing and child-ren laugh end - less - ly, for Christ-mas is fam - ily and

voic - es sing out mer-i - ly, of joy and turk - ey stuffed full and carols sung out of

75
G F G F G
End
C G
key.
Please take my hand
dar-ling let's go
80
Em F G Am hold
home.
83

Loneliest Time Of The Year

Lyrics by
Richard Mousseau

Score by
Richard Mousseau

It's that time of year, I do dread and fear. Knowing that I will hear greet-ings of good cheer. Sil-ver bells that ring, sweet voic-es that sing, hope and joy they bring is just not my thing. This is the lone-li-est time of the year, for those that have no one to hold so dear. False smiles that we pre-sent when we do miss a lov-ing kiss be-neath mis-le-toe.

Copyright December 11, 2019, Moose Hide Publishing
imprint of Moose Enterprise Book and Theatre Play Publishing
All rights reserved
684 Walls Rd. Prince Twp., Ontario Canada P6A 6K4
mooseenterprises@on.aibn.com www.moosehidebooks.com

40 G Am D C 2
46 C V 3 G Am
With a fire a - glow and Hall-mark Christ-mas shows, they pull at my heart -
51 D C V 4
strings. past mem-ories they will bring. I will shed a tear
56 G Am D
when no one is near, and hope that joy will bloom for those with Christ-mas
61 C Chorus D
gloom. This is the lone - li-est time of the year, for those that have
67 C
no one to hold so dear. False smiles that we pre-sent when we do
73 D Em C V 5
miss a lov-ing kiss be - neath mis-le - toe. In my heart I
79 G Am
love snow-flakes from a - bove. Sil - ver bells that ring, and

84 | D   C   V 6   G   3

sweet voic - es that sing. In my child - like heart Santa will do his

89 | Am   D   C

part bringing hope and joy each year, and some -one to hold dear.

94 | Chorus   D

This is the lone - li -est time of the year, for those that have no one

100 | C   End fade out

to hold so dear.

105 | D   Em   C

Santa, Did You Read My Letter?

Lyrics by
Richard Mousseau

Score by
Richard Mousseau

♩=120 *Christmas song*

Intro

(Boy & Girl) All I want for Christ-mas un-der-neath a tree, is a gift that will last, some-thing just for me. (Boy) I don't need those play toys like the oth-er boys. All that I would wish for, a gift I will a-dore. (Boy & Girl)

Chorus
San-ta did you read my let-ter sent by air-mail? I on-ly wish one gift to bring. If I am a good kid, you will not fail.

On this Christ-mas just one thing, some-one to love.

Copyright December 19, 2019, Moose Hide Publishing
imprint of Moose Enterprise Book and Theatre Play Publishing
All rights reserved
684 Walls Rd. Prince Twp., Ontario Canada P6A 6K4
mooseenterprises@on.aibn.com www.moosehidebooks.com

Lyrics under the staves:

(Boy & Girl) San-ta did you read my let - ter sent by air - mail?

I on-ly wish one gift to bring. If I am a good kid, you will not

fail. On this Christ-mas just one thing, some - one to love. (Girl)

I don't need a doll with curls like the oth - er girls. All that I would

wish for, a gift I will a - dore. (Boy & Girl) All I want for Christ - mas un - der -neath a

tree, is a gift that will last, par -ents just for me. San-ta did you read my

let - ter sent by air - mail? I on -ly wish one gift to bring.

88

C · Am · Dm · G · C · Am · G

If I am a good kid, you will not fail. On this Christ-mas just one

94

C · Am · G · C

thing, some - one to love. On this Christ - mas

98

Am · G · C · Am · G · C---- · Caug----- C⁶----------

please, please bring some - one to love.

Santa, Please Read My Letter

Lyrics by
Richard Mousseau

Score by
Richard Mousseau

Lyrics:

All I want for Christ - mas un - der-neath my tree, is a gal to hold tight some-one just for me. I don't need no more ties like the oth - er guys. All that I do wish for, a gal I can a - dore.

San-ta please read my let - ter sent by snail - mail? I on-ly crave just one old thing. If you know how I feel you will not fail. On this Christ-mas will you bring, some - one to love.

Copyright September 30, 2021, Moose Hide Publishing
imprint of Moose Enterprise Book and Theatre Play Publishing
All rights reserved
684 Walls Rd. Prince Twp., Ontario Canada P6A 6K4
mooseenterprises@on.aibn.com www.moosehidebooks.com

2

San-ta please read my let - ter sent by snail - mail? I on-ly crave

just one old thing. If you know how I feel you will not fail.

On this Christ-mas will you bring, some - one to love.

Please don't bring a blow - up doll from the sex shop mall. All that I do

wish for, a gal I can a - dore. Yes I'm just an old guy in an old folks

place. Yes it's so damn lone - ly no one to em - brace.

San-ta please read my let - ter sent by snail - mail? I on-ly crave just one old thing.   If you know how I feel   you will not   fail.

On this Christ-mas   will   you   bring,   some - one   to   love.

On   this Christ - mas   please   please   bring,

some - one   to   love.

Snow Flake Waltz

Lyrics by
Richard Mousseau

Score by
Richard Mousseau

Snow falkes fall-ing on a wint-er's morn. Fac-es smil-ing on a

beauti-ful day. Coup-les rid-ing through a wint-er's night, when star lights

dance an-d play. They first met on a storm-y night, at the town hall's sleigh ride dance.

They locked eyes from a-far, wish-ing to take a hope-fu-l chance. Slow-ly

twirl-ing a-round the dance hall floor. Arm in ar-m,

sway-ing to-geth-er for ev-e-r more.

Copyright November 27, 1975, Moose Hide Publishing
imprint of Moose Enterprise Book and Theatre Play Publishing
All rights reserved
684 Walls Rd. Prince Twp., Ontario Canada P6A 6K4
mooseenterprises@on.aibn.com www.moosehidebooks.com

Long cold wint - ers have passed by, and the sea - sons have changed with time. They still wait for wint-er snow, when sliegh bells be - gin to - chime.

They first met on a storm-y night, at the town hall's sleigh ride dance. They locked eyes from a - far, wish-ing to take a hope-fu - l chance. Grow-ing old ain`t no fun but as long as snow flakes fall, mom and dad will waltz a - gain a - round the floor at the old tow-n hall. Slow - ly twirl - ing a - round the dance hall floor. Arm in ar - m, sway-ing to-geth-er for ev - e - r more. Slow - ly twirl - ing a -

83

Dm   G⁷   F   C

round the dance hall floor.   Arm   in   ar - m,   sway-ing to-geth-er for

88 G⁷   C   G⁷   C

ev - e - r more.   sway - ing to - geth - er   for   ev - e - r more.

91

They Tell Me this is Christmass

Lyrics by
Richard Mousseau

Score by
Richard Mousseau

They tell me this is christ-mass, it hap-pens once a year, when snow is fall-ing, hearts are of good cheer. ring-ing, ring-ing, sleigh-bells, are ring - ing. They tell me this is christ-mass, with vis-ions of child - hood, writ - ting to san-ta, prom-ising to be good. ring-ing, ring-ing, sleigh-bells, are ring - ing.

Copyright December 24, 2016, Moose Hide Publishing
imprint of Moose Enterprise Book and Theatre Play Publishing
All rights reserved
684 Walls Rd. Prince Twp., Ontario Canada P6A 6K4
mooseenterprises@on.aibn.com www.moosehidebooks.com

I've been wonder -ing

what will be, if this world will ev -er see, has

an -y bod -y seen good -will at all this year?

v 4
World wide news will bring dis -dain, ever -y word is a re -frian,

has an -y bod -y seen good -will at all this year?

v 1
They tell me this is christ -mass, it hap -pens once a year, when

snow is fall -ing, hearts are of good cheer. ring -ing, ring -ing,

bridge
sleigh -bells, are ring - ing.

Will you help your good neigh-bour, off - er them a real fa-vour,

will an - y bod - y see good-will at all this year?

Off - er each a help-ing hand, spread good will a -

cross this land, will an y bod y see good-will at all this

year? They tell me this is christ -mass, it

hap -pens once a year, when snow is fall-ing, hearts are of good cheer. ring-ing,

ring-ing, sleigh-bells, are ring - ing. They tell me this is christ -mass, with

vis -ions of child - hood, writ - ting to san -ta, prom -ising to be good. ring-ing, ring -ing,   sleigh -bells,   are   ring   -   ing.

When Hearts Believe

Lyrics by
Richard Mousseau

Score by
Richard Mousseau

The north wind blows win-ter snows and warm hearts are a-glow when lov-ers em-brace be-neath mis-tle-toe.

Hear the bells ring voice-s sing, 'Auld Lang Syne.' Dreams come true when hearts be-lieve on New-Years Eve.

Give a kiss to your girl and a hug to your guy, it's a love a-fair young ones want to try. Hear the bells ring voice-s sing, 'Auld Lang Syne.' Dreams come true when hearts be-lieve on New-Years Eve.

Copyright April 10, 2015, Moose Hide Publishing
imprint of Moose Enterprise Book and Theatre Play Publishing
All rights reserved
684 Walls Rd. Prince Twp., Ontario Canada P6A 6K4
mooseenterprises@on.aibn.com www.moosehidebooks.com

See the light of fire glow in a cabin wrapped in snow when young hearts whis-per these words all should know. Hear the bells ring voice-s sing, 'Auld Lang Syne.' Dreams come true when hearts be-lieve on New-Years Eve. Hear the bells ring voice-s sing, 'Auld Lang Syne.'

www.ingramcontent.com/pod-product-compliance
Lightning Source LLC
Chambersburg PA
CBHW081547040426
42448CB00015B/3253

9 781927 393710